BY
B C BOYER

MARLOWE & COMPANY
NEW YORK

First printing, 1996

Published by
Marlowe & Company
632 Broadway, Seventh Floor
New York, New York 10012

http://www.marlowepub.com

ISBN 1-56924-757-9

Printed in Canada

EDITED BY CAT YRONWODE

HEARTBREAK NEWS

CHAPTER 1

A BLOSSOM BY ANY OTHER NAME

For

Charles Boyer,

who took his son
under his arm
and taught him how
to draw a line.

I APPRECIATE YOU COMING *ALL THIS WAY*, MR. BACH . BUT . . . MY FATHER'S BEEN ALONE *ALL THIS TIME*. I DON'T KNOW IF I COULD . . .

HOW ABOUT GREEN EGGS AND HAM.

NO!

THANK-YOU!

I WOULD *NOT* LIKE *GREEN EGGS* AND *HAM!*

NOT *HERE!* NOT *THERE!* NOT ANYWHERE!

NOW, HILLY. *I* DON'T WANT YOU TO STAY JUST BECAUSE OF . . . *ME* . . .

NO FATHER . IT'S NOT THAT . . .

SOUP?

NO! THANK-YOU! NOT SOUP! NOT GREEN EGGS AND HAM! NOT ANYTHING! I DON'T WANT ANYTHING BUT WATER! YOU GOT THAT?!

AHEM!

YED.

WELL DOW.

WHAT CAD I GET YOU, MIDDER STEEL TRAB~

-OBBS!

UH. . *PLUCK* ME CAREFULLY, WILL YOU PLEASE. I'M. . . HAVING A BAD DAY.

WAIT! WHY DON'T YOU GIVE US JUST A *COUPLE* OF *MINUTES*, OKAY?

YES MA'AM. THANK-YOU, MA'AM. MY LIFE IS OVER, MA'AM.

IT ALL SOUNDS SO *EXCITING*, MR. BACH. I. . .JUST CAN'T DECIDE. I DON'T WANT TO *JUMP* INTO SOMETHING I'M NOT *READY* FOR.

YOUR TALENTS *FAR SURPASS* WHAT *EVER* STORIES THIS *BACKWOODS* PLANET CAN *MUSTER*. WE NEED YOU ON *EARTH*. THINGS ARE *HAPPENING* THERE.

LIKE I *SAID* . . . THERE'S *PLENTY* OF *ACTION* HERE FOR HILLY TO COVER.

COFFEE?

RRRRRRRRRRRRR

WHAT'S THAT *RUMBLING* SOUND?

LOOKS LIKE SOMEONE'S TRYING TO *CRASH* TROUGH THE. . .

CCCRRCRRACH

YEEEOOOW!

WEASEL CALHOON
AND VERMIN LECROY

EDITED BY CAT YRONWODE

HEARTBREAK NEWS

CHAPTER 2

WEASEL CALHOON AND VERMIN LECROY

SILVIA, HOLD MY CALLS!

TELL HIM I'LL GET *BACK* TO HIM.

THREE MESSAGES, CHIEF. INCLUDING THE *GOVERNOR.*

NEW EDITION, CHIEF!

EXCELLENT! AND OUT IN *FORTY MINUTES* TOO!

YOU SAW IT *LIVE,* LADIES AND GENTLEMEN. . .RIGHT HERE AT *CHAPMAN'S BAR* AND *GRILLE!*

C'MERE, BOSS. I'VE GOT SOMETHING TO *SHOW* YOU.

NOT NOW, CHEMICALS. I'M *BUSY!*

IT'LL JUST TAKE A *MINUTE.* IT'S *IMPORTANT!*

TA DA! SEE! IT'S *ALL DONE!*

THE *SPECIAL PACKAGE!* YOU'RE DONE *BUILDING IT?*

YESSIR! ALL ACCORDING TO *SPECIFICATIONS*

CAREFUL AROUND THERE, HARV.

DON'T WORRY. HE'S GOT A *BRAIN* THE SIZE OF A *WALNUT.*

BUT THAT *SPECIAL PACKAGE* TOOK ME A *LONG TIME* TO *BUILD!*

HORRIBLE!

DO YOU *REALIZE* YOUR MAN *SIDNEY* CAME *BUSTING* IN WHILE MY *DAUGHTER* AND I WERE *THERE?!?!?*

YOU WANTED JEAN CLAUDE SILENCED.

BUT *NOT* WHILE *I'M* THERE!

WHERE *DID* YOU GET THAT *CRAZY CHARACTER, ANYWAY?*

I HAVE MY MEANS.

HE *DIDN'T* EVEN *KILL* JEAN CLAUDE!

THE KID'S STILL LEARNING.

I WANT JEAN CLUDE *DEAD!* IF HE *SPILLS* THE *BEANS* ABOUT MY *PAYOFFS*...

I'LL TAKE CARE OF HIM.

I *CERTAINLY HOPE* MY *BANKROLL* IS SUPPORTING *A LOT MORE* THAN JUST THAT *ROOKIE!*

OFCOURSE. AS A MATTER OF FACT, I SHOULD INTRODUCE YOU TO MY *OTHER* ASSOCIATES.

ALL RIGHT BOYS... *TRANSPORT* TO COORDINATES *G-H, PAGE THIRTY TWO* OF THE *THOMAS GUIDE.*

AND ME . . .

I'LL BE ALONE . . .

. . . ONCE AGAIN.

THIS 'ERE MUST BE ONE O' THEM, WHUTCHACALL, *REFLECTIVE MOMENTS.*

YEAH . . . LIKE SAY YER *EVIL,* YUH KNOW . . . 'N YUH STARTS TUH SHOW YER *SOFT* SIDE . . .

SOFT IS *GOOD.*

SOFT IS *VERY* GOOD.

YOU *SURE* WE CAN *TRUST* THIS GUY?

DON'T WORRY. NO ONE *EVER* BELIEVES HIM *HEH. HEH.*

AND *WHAT* HAVE WE *HERE?*

NAME'S *WEASEL CALHOON.* THIS 'ERE'S MUH *LONG TIME 'SOCIATE 'N' CLOSE* COMPANION, VERMIN LECROY.

CLOSE, HUH? .HMMM. AND YOU'RE *SINGLE ...THIN ...*

STAY BACK! JUS' TWO FEET...THAT'S *ALL* I ASK!

JUST *TWO FEET!*

OH *BACH!* BLOSSOM DIDN'T *MEAN* TO HURT YOU .

I'M SURE SHE *DIDN'T.* IT WAS AN *UNCONSCIOUS* THING.

SHE HAS AN *INBORN TALENT* FOR MAKIN' ME *UNCONSCIOUS!*

LISTEN...WE NEED TO GET SOME *INFORMATION* ON THIS *JEAN-CLAUDE* FELLA.IT'S THE *ONLY* LEAD WE'VE *GOT.*

THIS IS ALL SO *EXCITIN* MISS HILLY. I *KNEW* IT WOULD BE GREAT!

UH ... BLOSSOM . WOULD YOU LIKE TO *HELP* ME?

SURE!

NEXT...

BROKEN TRUST

EDITED BY CAT YRONWODE

HEARTBREAK NEWS

CHAPTER 3

BROKEN TRUST

THEY'RE NOT?

NO!

WHAT *ARE* THEY?

JUST...UH...A *NEW LOOK!* THAT'S ALL!...*FOR MY COSTUME*... DESIGNED TO STRIKE *FEAR* INTO THE HEARTS OF MY *VICTIMS!!*

IT DOESN'T DO ANYTHING FOR ME.

OF COURSE NOT!! YOU'RE AN *EVILDOER!* YOU GET *OFF* ON FEAR!!

TRUE. TRUE. STILL...WHEN I FINISH MY GREAT GALACTIC *NOVEL* ABOUT THE WAYS AND MEANS OF *KILLING* PEOPLE...

I'D PROBABLY BRING A BIT OF *LEVITY* TO IT ...JUST TO LET FOLKS KNOW IT'S NOT ALL A *DRUDGERY.*

AN IN-DEPTH STUDY
OF THE VERY DEEP
THINKING MR. HARV

EDITED BY CAT YRONWODE

HEARTBREAK NEWS

CHAPTER 4

AN INDEPTH STUDY OF THE VERY DEEP THINKING MR. HARV

MY FATHER TRIED TO BE A ROLE MODEL BY SHOWING THE IMPORTANCE OF BEING PART OF ORGANIZATIONS.

PASS THE GRAVY.

MOTHER, FOR HER PART, TRIED TO INSPIRE IN ME A VIVID IMAGINATION BY ACTING OUT BED-TIME STORIES.

RED RIDING HOOD *SCREAMED* AS THE WOODSMAN *WHACKED* THE WOLF TO *PIECES*.

NO! NO! DON'T HIT SPOT! YOU'RE HURTING HIM!!!

WHACK! WHACK! WHACK! WHACK!

AND SO I GREW UP THINKING OF THE STRANGE AND MORBID AS QUITE NORMAL.

NICE LAMP, DEAR.

YEAH. WELL MAYBE *NEXT* TIME THE *FEDERAL EXPRESS MAN* WON'T DAMAGE MY *PACKAGES*.

I THOUGHT BEING DRAFTED WOULD HELP ME IN MY TRYING TO BE PART OF SOCIETY.

KILL! KILL! KILL!

IT ONLY FANNED THE FLAMES OF WHATEVER DARKSIDE I WAS HOLDING BACK.

WHEN IT CAME TIME TO FACING THE UNDERBELLY OF DEBAUCHERY BY ELIMINATING VILLAGES ON JANUS FOUR, MY COLLEGES WERE HESITANT.. BEING WEIGHTED DOWN BY SOMETHING THEY GREW UP WITH... SOMETHING THEY CALLED... CONSCIENCE.

I, HOWEVER, TRIED MY BEST TO SHOW I WAS A PART OF SOCIETY BY FULFILLING MY RESPONSIBILITIES.

THE CONSEQUENCES OFWHICH LATER LED TO MY CONVICTION.

IT WAS THEN I REALIZED WHAT MY PURPOSE WAS.

AND WHAT MY GREAT GALACTIC NOVEL SHOULD BE ALL ABOUT.

WHEN I WAS PAROLED, I WENT ABOUT TRYING TO FIND MORE INFORMATION ON THIS CONSCIENCE THING.

OH. NOW DON'T *DECEIVE* YOURSELF, STEELTRAP.

MY QUEST IS *NOT* TO OBTAIN A *CONSCIENCE.*

NO.

FAR FROM IT.

MY JOURNEY IS TO PROVE THERE'S *NO SUCH THING.* THAT I AM *JUST* AS NORMAL AS *EVERYBODY* ELSE.

THAT *EVERYBODY* IN THE *WORLD...*

IS *JUST LIKE ME.*

AND AT THE *END* OF THE ROAD...OF ALL THIS *HAVOC* AND *DESTRUCTION...*

YOU, ROSE, WILL *BE* THERE...

WITH ME...

WITH *NARY* A CONSCIENCE BLOWING IN THE WIND.

AND WHILE WE STAND THERE...

YOU'LL **LOOK** AT ME IN THE *EYE*...

AND SEE...

YOUR SOUL.

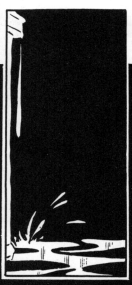

IS IT WORTH IT?

IS IT?

YOU TELL ME.

AW, *CHIEF*. HE DIDN'T *MEAN* IT.

HE MUST'VE BEEN *ABUSED* AS A CHILD.

IT'S NOT *HIS* FAULT.

GIVE HIM A *BREAK*, CHIEF.

I CAN'T *BELIEVE* YOU GUYS! AFTER *ALL* HE'S *DONE*.

SO HE *GOOFED UP*. WHO *HASN'T*?

NO! I CAN'T

I *CAN'T* GO BACK ON MY WORD!! I *CAN'T!*

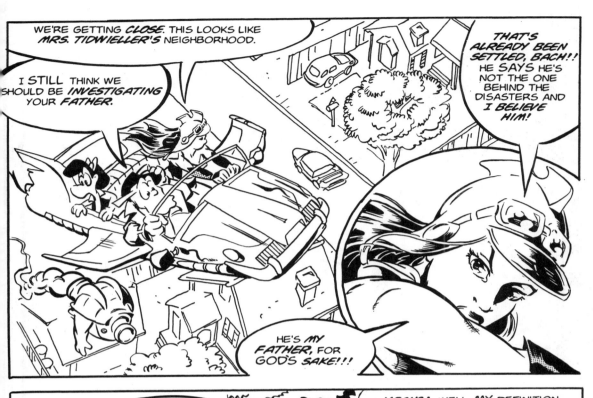

WE'RE GETTING *CLOSE*. THIS LOOKS LIKE *MRS. TIDWIELLER'S* NEIGHBORHOOD.

I STILL THINK WE SHOULD BE *INVESTIGATING* YOUR *FATHER*.

THAT'S ALREADY BEEN SETTLED, BACH!! HE SAYS HE'S NOT THE ONE BEHIND THE DISASTERS AND *I BELIEVE HIM!*

HE'S *MY FATHER*, FOR GOD'S *SAKE!!!*

A GOOD REPORTER INVESTIGATES ALL ANGLES.. EVEN AT THE *RISK* OF LOSING *EVERYTHING!*

INCLUDING *RELATIONSHIPS!*

YEAH?! WELL *MY* DEFINITION INCLUDES BEING *HUMAN* FIRST...

A *VULTURE* SECOND.

THIS IS THE PLACE.

WELL, HILLY. I *HATE* TO BE THE *FIRST* TO DESTROY YOUR *ETHICAL BUBBLE*...

F RING F RING F

BUT *REACHING* THE *PROFESSIONAL LEVEL* INVOLVES *TENACITY*...

INTEGRITY... CLASS...

POINT!

AN INTERESTING PLOT
DEVELOPEMENT REGARDING
MRS. TIDWIELLER AND HER SON

EDITED BY CAT YRONWODE

HEARTBREAK NEWS

CHAPTER 5

AN INTERESTING PLOT DEVELOPMENT REGARDING MRS. TIDWHIELLER AND HER SON

MRS.TIDWIELLER! THERE'S SOME *GUESTS* WHO WOULD LIKE TO *SEE* YOU.

REALLY?

I HAVEN'T HAD *VISITORS* IN *SUCH* A LONG TIME. PLEASE COME IN. HAVE A SEAT. CAN WE GET YOU ANYTHING?

THANK YOU, MRS.TIDWIELLER.

NURSE PRACHETT?

YES, MUM. IT'LL JUST BE A MINUTE, MUM.

OOOOH MY! YOU'RE SOOOOO *PRECIOUS!*

THANK YOU, MA'AM.

UNGG

LET ME THINK NOW. IS *CHOKING* SOMETHING SO PRECIOUS A *BAD* THING

TO WHAT DO I *OWE* THIS *PLEASURE?*

WELL, I DON'T KNOW IF YOU *REMEMBER*... BUT WHEN I WAS A *LITTLE GIRL,* YOU ALWAYS GAVE US KIDS IN THE NEIGHBORHOOD *MILK* AND *COOKIES!*

I DON'T RECALL SPECIFICALLY. .BUT I *DO* HAVE *FOND MEMORIES* OF THE NEIGHBORHOOD *CHILDREN.*

MY NAME'S *HILLY ROSE*... BUT THEN, YOU MIGHT NOT REMEMBER. I WAS JUST *ONE* OF THE *KIDS.*

ACTUALLY. . . IT WAS MOSTLY BOYS WHO CAME BY. .BEING AS I HAD A SON AND ALL. THERE WERE VERY FEW GIRLS.

I *LOVED* YOUR *DESSERTS.* THEY WERE *DELIGHTFUL.* I GOT A *COUPLE* OF *RECIPES* FOR MY *MOM.*

THEY WERE HANDED DOWN TO ME FROM MY *MOTHER*. . .AND FROM HERS. HOW'D THEY *WORK OUT?*

UH. . .

WELL. . .MY MOM WAS SO *BUSY,* YOU KNOW.

SHE WOULD'VE *COOKED UP* A BATCH IF SHE'D *HAD TIME.* I *KNOW* SHE WOULD'VE.

I DO SEEM TO RECALL A LITTLE GIRL. . .SORT OF A *TOM BOY*. . .STRAGGLY HAIR. . .

COULD'VE USED A *WASH.*

BOTH HER PARENTS *WORKED.* THEY WERE *EVER* HOME. SO SHE HUNG AROUND THE *NEIGHBORHOOD* A LOT.

SOMETIMES SHE'D EVEN *HELP* ME *COOK.*

HEH. I REMEMBER ONE TIME. . .I *DOLLED* HER UP *REAL PRETTY-LIKE*. . .SEWED HER A *DRESS*. . .PUT HER *HAIR* IN *PIGTAILS.*

I. . .KEPT IT THAT WAY FOR *MONTHS.*

SHE REALLY LOOKED LIKE A *FINE YOUNG LADY.*

SIGFIELD

NOW LOOK WHAT YOU'VE *DONE!* THE MISSUS IS *UPSET!*

AW, *SHUT* YER *YAP,* LADY! IT'S MY *JOB!* THIS IS WHAT I *DO! SHEESH!*

I'M SORRY, MRS. TIDWIELLER. IS THERE ANYTHING I CAN--

OH NO, DEAR. BELIEVE ME. . .I'M *USED* TO IT BY NOW. I'VE SEEN HIM LIKE THAT *BEFORE.*

SO. . *SIDNEY* IS IN FACT, YOUR SON, *SIDFIELD.*

YES.

AND NOW. . .IT'S *YOUR* TURN. WHAT WILL IT BE ? COFFEE, TEA , OR *PUNCH?!!*

OH, NO! I KNOW WHAT YOU'RE GOING TO *DO.*

I'VE SEEN ALL THE CARTOONS. I KNO[W] WHAT YOU'LL DO IF I SAY *I* WANT PUNCH

I'M *WAY* AHEAD OF YA, *NURSE, PRACHETT!* I'LL TAKE TEA!

OH, DEAR.

AND IT'S SO *HOT,* TOO!

STRANGER! I NEED YOU, FAST!

COME HERE!

YES?

MY DAUGHTER! HILLY! YOU TRIED TO KILL HER!

WHAT?

HER SPECIAL PACKAGE! YOU SABOTAGE IT!

YOU TOLD ME TO!

I TOLD YOU TO MAKE SURE IT FOLLOWS OUR ORDERS!

I DIDN'T TELL YOU TO RIG IT SO IT WOULD KILL HER. IT WENT BUCK WILD!

THIS CONTRAPTION MADE IT GO HAYWIRE!

DANG. THAT GUY AT RADIO SHACK SAID--

I DON'T CARE WHAT HE SAID!

MY DAUGHTER IS MY LIFE!!!

IF YOU HURT EVEN A HAIR ON HER HEAD, IT'S OVER!!

YOU GOT THA—ARGH!!

NO ONE... TOUCHES... MY SERAPE.

THAWK!

WHY'D YOUR SON HAVE A *TROUBLED CHILDHOOD?*

OH, IT'S REALLY A SAD STORY.

YOU SEE... WHEN SIGFIELD FIRST CAME INTO THE WORLD, HE WAS BORN WITH A *BIRTH DEFECT.*

A BIRTH DEFECT?

UUGGH?

YES. HE WAS BORN WITHOUT EARS.

OH, HE COULD *HEAR* ALL RIGHT-- BUT *ALL* HE HAD WAS A *FOLD* OF *SKIN*.

NEEDLESS TO SAY, ALL THE CHILDREN MADE *FUN* OF HIM. HE GREW UP *HATING LIFE*. . .AND EVERYONE HE ENCOUNTERED.

I TRIED TO COMFORT HIM...HOLD HIM *CLOSE*. . .AS ONLY A *MOTHER* COULD.

BUT. . .≤SIGH≥. . .HE REJECTED ME, TOO, FOR *BRINGING* HIM INTO THE *WORLD* WITH SUCH A *DEFORMITY*.

FINALLY, ONE DAY, WHEN HE WAS *TWELVE*, TWO *SOCIAL WORKERS* CAME BY.

THEY OFFERED HIM an *OPERATION.*

THEY SAID THEY'D *FOUND* A DONOR FOR HIS EARS. HE COULD *RECEIVE* A *TRANSPLANT.*

≤SIGH≥ HE ACCEPTED THE OPERATION, NOT WITH *GRATITUDE,* BUT WITH *BITTERNESS...*

...IN EFFECT SAYING, "IT'S ABOUT *TIME* YOU GAVE ME WHAT I *SHOULD HAVE HAD* ALL ALONG."

I WAS SO *DISAPPOINTED.*

OH, DEAR. THERE SEEMS TO BE A *FLY* AMISS. NURSE PRACHETT?

YES, MUM.

WOULD YOU BE SO KIND AS TO *TAKE CARE* OF IT FOR ME?

YES, MUM?

NASTY LITTLE THINGS, *DON'T* YOU *THINK?*

ANYWAY. . . WHERE WAS I ?

OH, YES. . .SIGFIELD. HE WAS STILL A *BITTER YOUNG MAN.*

RUMBLE

RUMBLE

RUMBLE

RUMBLE

RUMBLE

HE NEVER DID MAKE PEACE WITH HIMSELF.

I FELT SO BAD.

POOF
POOF
POOF

SHOOO! SHOOOO!

HAVE SOME CRUMPETS!

≤SIGH≥ I HAVEN'T HEARD FROM HIM *SINCE!*

BUT NOW. . .I GUESS HE'S GOTTEN INTO *CRIME.*

IF I HAVE ANY MORE QUESTIONS, MAY I COME BACK?

OF COURSE.

SHE SURE IS A *NICE LADY.*

WE MUST COME AGAIN. EVEN IF IT'S JUST TO *STOP* AND SAY *HI.*

ALRIGHT, STRANGER!! LISTEN!!!

I DON'T LIKE YOU *JEOPARDIZING* THE LIFE OF MY *DAUGHTER!*

IT BOILS DOWN TO *THIS.* I'M PAYING YOU TO *COMMIT* THESE CRIMES 'N' I CAN HANG YOU *OUT* TO *DRY* IN A *SECOND!!*

YOU TURN ME IN. . .YOU'RE GOING DOWN *WITH* ME.

I DON'T CARE. I'VE GOT NOTHING TO LOSE.

BUT YOU. . .

. . .YOU'VE GOT A *CAREER.* . . A *GOOD NAME.*

ACKNOWLEDGMENTS

I'd like to thank my wife. sweet Sandra D..
my kids Brandon. Bria
and Brodie.
I'd also like to thank
Robert Cox
Kaye Reshaw
Richard Reshaw
Bart Boyer
My Mom and Sister
and the rest of my family and friends for all their support.

In the industry I'd like to thank
Cat Yronwode. Dave Sim. Batton Lash. Jackie Estrada.
Micheal Cohen. Randy Reynaldo. James Eisele.
Barry Short. Paul Lazear. Chris Peterson. Don Simpson.
Jim Valentino. Kurt Busiek. James Owens. Marcus Harwell.
Teri Wood. Mark Herr. Glen Fallen. Mark Evanier. William Tucci.
all the comicbook stores who support me
and the fans who reccomend
Hilly Rose to their friends.

YOU'VE JUST READ ISSUES #1-5 OF HILLY ROSE.
IF YOU'D LIKE TO READ MORE OF HER ADVENTURES
LOOK IN YOUR PHONE BOOK FOR A COMICBOOK STORE
NEAR YOU.

OR YOU CAN
SUBSCRIBE
TODAY BY
FILLING
OUT THE
FORM
BELOW.
EACH ISSUE
IS 32 PAGES
OF BLACK
AND WHITE
INTERIOR
WITH
COLOR
COVERS.

SEND CHECK OR MONEY ORDER
PAYABLE IN U.S. FUNDS TO:

☐ HILLY ROSE --- $3.50 EACH

☐ SIX ISSUE SUBSCRIPTION --- $18.00

☐ TWELVE ISSUE SUBSCRIPTION - $36.00

☐ PAPERBACK VOL. 1 (ISSUES 1-5) $12.95

Outside the U.S and Canada add $1.50 per book for postage

ASTRO COMICS
4195 CHINO HILLS PKWY
SUITE 329
CHINO HILLS , CA.
91709

ROCKET TIMES

AUG 24, 2995
VOLUME 95 ISSUE 47

15 CREDITS

20 CREDITS IN THE RALON SECTOR